D1091098

GYMNASTICS

By
Newt Loken
Gymnastic Coach, University of Michigan

ATHLETIC INSTITUTE SERIES

STERLING PUBLISHING CO., Inc.   **New York**

Foreword

"Gymnastics" is but one item in a comprehensive list of sports instruction aids made available on a non-profit basis by The Athletic Institute. The photographic material in this book has been reproduced in total from The Athletic Institute's sound, color slidefilm, "Beginning Apparatus Activities." This book and the slidefilm are parts of a program designed to bring the many benefits of athletics, physical education and recreation to everyone.

The Athletic Institute is a non-profit organization devoted to the advancement of athletics, physical education and recreation. It functions on the premise that athletics and recreation bring benefits of inestimable value to the individual and to the community.

The nature and scope of the many Institute programs are determined by an advisory committee of selected persons noted for their outstanding knowledge, experience and ability in the fields of athletics, physical education and recreation.

It is their hope, and the hope of the Institute, that through this book, the reader will become a better apparatus activities participant, skilled in the fundamentals of this fine sport. Knowledge, and the practice necessary to mold knowledge into actual ability, are the keys to real enjoyment of apparatus activities.

CONTENTS

ONE—PARALLEL BARS.. 5
    Dip 6
    Swing 7
    Straddle Seat 8
    Front Support Turn... 9
    Side Seat Half Turn to Straddle Seat.......................... 11
    Top Kip to Straddle Seat.. 12
    Shoulder Balance 14
    Backward Straddle Shoulder Roll................................. 16
    Back Uprise 18
    Dismounts 20
TWO—HORIZONTAL BAR.. 23
    Grips 24
    Front Support Mount... 26
    Back Dismount 27
    Skin the Cat.. 28
    Single Knee Swing-Up and Circles.............................. 29
    Back Hip Circle 31
    Kip 33
    Double Leg Circle Backward.. 36
    Sole Circle Backward.. 38
THREE—RINGS 41
    Chin-Ups 42
    Skin the Cat.. 44
    Bird's Nest 45
    Kip to Straight Arm Support... 47
    Dislocate 49
    Inlocate 51
    Back Uprise 52
    Reverse Kip 53
    Flying Rings 55
    Flyaway 56
FOUR—SIDE HORSE EXERCISES.. 58
    Leg Circles 62
    Reverse Scissors 67
    Right Feint 69
    Single Rear Dismount 69
    Flank Circles 70
    Double Rear Dismount.. 72
    Triple Rear Dismount.. 74
FIVE—SIDE HORSE AND LONG HORSE VAULTING...................... 78
    Side Horse Vaults... 79
    Neckspring 87
    Long Horse Vaults.. 91
    Handstand Cartwheel 94
    Handspring 95

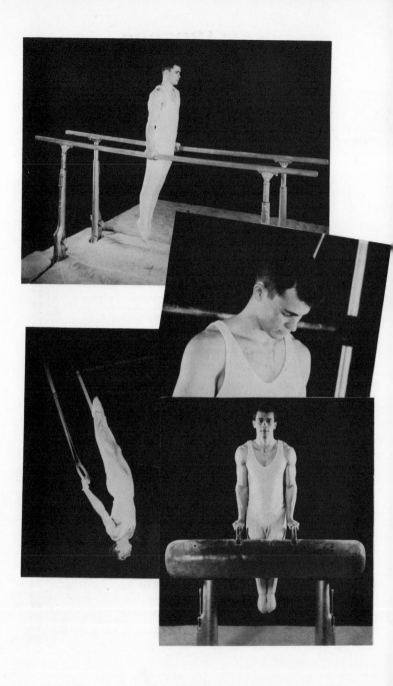

PARALLEL BARS

Becoming a successful performer on the parallel bars takes more than strength and some tumbling experience. You must be willing to devote a lot of time to practice, building your skill and confidence gradually.

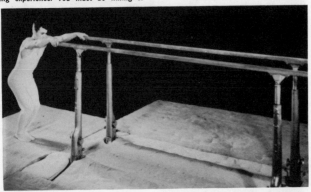

First familiarize yourself with the apparatus. The parallel bars are two smooth wooden handrails supported on a pair of sturdy uprights and bases. For safety's sake the base area should be padded with mats . . .

. . . and the bars adjusted to about chest height while you're learning. First, get the feel of the bars, using a basic overhand grip. Then develop a good approach . . .

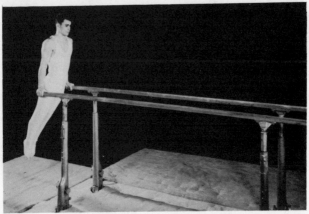

. . . and a simple starting mount such as the jump to a straight arm support. Practice until you can support yourself with your arms

straight, chest out, body slightly arched and your toes pointing down. Once you've learned this basic mount . . .

DIP

. . . you can try a beginning stunt such as the Dip. After a jump to a straight arm support . . .

. . . flex your arms and ease yourself down low without touching the mat. Bend your arms to the point where they form slightly less than a right angle. Then push yourself back up . . .

. . . to your original straight arm support. Practice until you can do several dips in a row.

It's a good arm exercise and effective conditioning for your next basic movement . . .

SWING

...the Swing. Develop a high, strong swing only after many low, easy swings. Learn them with proper spotting for safety.

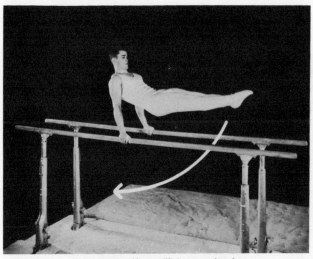

Soon you can add more lift to your swing. As you swing higher, keep your arms straight. Try to make your shoulders the fulcrum of your swing. You'll need a good swing to perfect another mount...

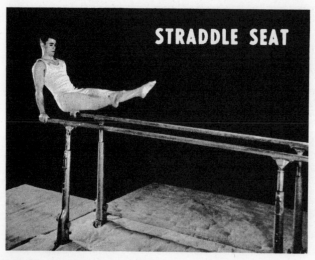

STRADDLE SEAT

...the Straddle Seat. Starting from a straight arm support, swing your legs forward. As they come up slightly above the bars . . .

...separate your legs and let each drop on a bar. Then sit up so you end in a straddle seat, your head up, your back and legs straight, and your hands resting behind you on the bars.

FRONT
SUPPORT TURN

The Front Support Turn is another stunt that begins with a straight arm support. Go into your support in the center of the bars.

Then, if you're going to turn to the right, lean to your right. Shift your weight and hips over to that side, and bring your left hand over to the right bar.

Shift your weight quickly to your left arm, supporting yourself for a moment with the front of your thighs resting against the bar. Keep your body straight and back slightly arched.

Then continue your half-turn by reaching back with your right hand to grip the other bar.

When you complete your turn, you'll finish in a straight arm support again, only facing the other way.

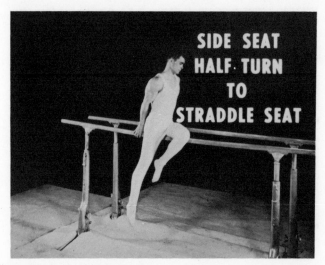

SIDE SEAT
HALF TURN
TO
STRADDLE SEAT

Another basic stunt in which you turn around
is the Side Seat Half Turn to Straddle Seat.
Start it from a side seat on one bar.

Then swing one leg over the bars, turning
yourself in that same direction and placing
your outside hand on the far bar. Complete
your half turn . . .

... and finish in a straddle seat position, with
your legs straight and hands resting on both
bars. Once you've mastered this stunt ...

... you can try another, such as the Top Kip
to Straddle Seat. Start this stunt in an upper
arm support with your legs raised overhead in
a pike position.

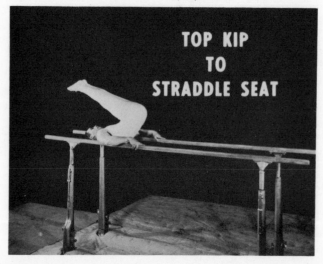

**TOP KIP
TO
STRADDLE SEAT**

12

Then roll your hips forward slightly, and quickly kick your legs forward and downward toward the bars, pulling with your arms at the same time. As you come forward . . .

. . . spread your legs and land in a straddle seat position. When you've perfected these basic stunts . . .

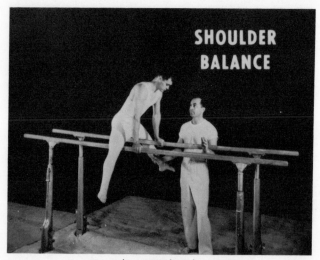

. . . you can try a more advanced one, such as
the Shoulder Balance. At first you'll need the
help of a spotter. Start from a straddle seat
and lean forward on both hands . . .

. . . until the bars support your upper arms
close to your shoulders. Your elbows are out
to the sides. Raise your hips, keeping your
legs extended, forcing your body straight up
over your head . . .

... into a shoulder balance ... back arched, toes pointed. Later on, after some practice, you can go on to a more advanced balance ...

SWING TO
SHOULDER BALANCE

... the Swing to a Shoulder Balance. From a straight arm support, swing back and forth a few times. At the end of a back swing, flex your arms ...

...and drop down so you support yourself on your upper arms. Continue to grip the bars with your hands, arch your back, and swing up to a straight shoulder balance. Later on ...

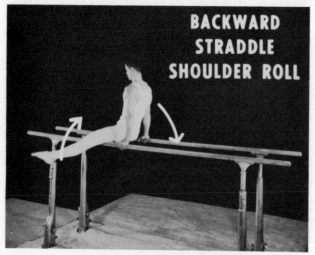

BACKWARD STRADDLE SHOULDER ROLL

...you can try the Backward Straddle Shoulder Roll. Begin it from a straddle seat, your hands gripping the bars behind you. Then lean backward ...

. . . and raise your legs, keeping them straight and spread out wide. Bring them over you as your arms and shoulders rest back on the bars. Now push with your arms . . .

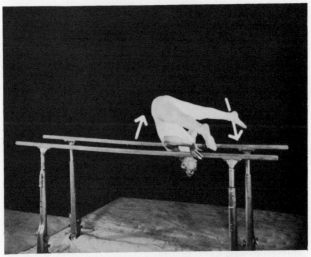

. . . roll back over your shoulders, and drop your spread legs down toward the bars again. During the roll, you'll have to let go of the bars and then re-grasp on the other side of your shoulders. As your legs come all the way over . . .

... push yourself up to an upright position and back in a straddle seat.

BACK UPRISE

Next you can try a Back Uprise. Make sure the bars are raised to regulation height. Start the Back Uprise with an upper arm support with your body in a kip position.

Now swing your legs down into a strong back swing.

At the peak of your back swing, take advantage of your momentum. Pull hard with the arms and straighten them so that you finish in a regular straight arm support. After you've perfected the Back Uprise, you'll want to develop a few dismounts. A good dismount will protect you from injury and give your performance a smart finish.

FRONT DISMOUNT

The first one you might try is the Front Vault Dismount. Start by swinging back from a straight arm support. At the peak of your back swing, if you're vaulting to the right, shift your weight over the right bar. Bring your left hand over at the same time. The instant you have a firm grip with your left hand, release your right . . .

. . . and drop to the mat, your left hand holding the bar to balance your landing. With practice, you can go on to a more impressive dismount . . .

REAR DISMOUNT

. . . a Rear Vault Dismount. At the peak of a forward swing, vault over one bar. Bring one hand over to grip the bar behind you. Then release the other hand as you land on the mat with your inside hand holding the bar.

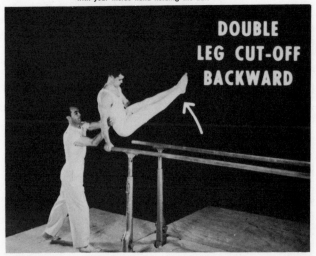

DOUBLE LEG CUT-OFF BACKWARD

Another dismount is the Double Leg Cut-off Backward. Swing both legs forward from a straight arm support position. As they swing above the bars, pass them over one bar and backward. Release the grip on that side and allow the legs to continue to swing backward toward the mats. Then drop to a standing position facing the bars with each hand on a bar.

STRADDLE FORWARD DISMOUNT

To do the Straddle Forward Dismount, swing your legs and hips backward, spread your feet outside the bars in a straddle, and shoot your legs forward, releasing your grip to drop to a landing. After perfecting these stunts individually ...

... you can concentrate on arranging them into routines, improving them by adding spectacular catches and somersaults. But remember that it takes a lot of training before you can arrive at this point ...

... the time when you will be a successful performer on the parallel bars.

2

HORIZONTAL BAR

If you've ever "skinned the cat" on a tree branch or porch railing, you'll know performing on the horizontal bar can be an exciting activity.

The horizontal bar itself is a simple apparatus. It's supported by two well-braced steel uprights from six to eight feet apart. And it can be adjusted from a full regulation height of eight feet down to three feet. You'll want to start out on the low horizontal bar, where it's set at shoulder height.

23

Test the bar to make sure it's securely adjusted. Check its surface for moisture, rust or pitting. You can keep the bar smooth by rubbing emery paper or steel wool over it at frequent intervals.

It's a good idea to protect your hands by wearing a pair of palm guards. These may be made of leather or lamp wicking. For further protection remember to first practice in short sessions until your hands have toughened up. Always remember to keep your hands well chalked to prevent slipping off.

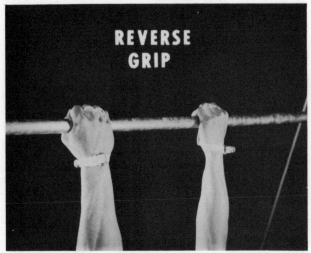

REVERSE GRIP

Now you can try out a few basic grips. One of them is the underhand or reverse grip, in which your hands circle the bar with the palms facing you.

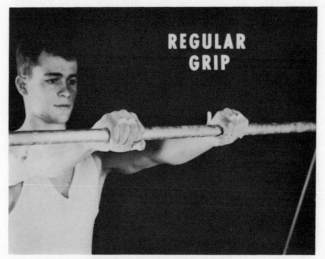

REGULAR GRIP

Another is the overhand or regular grip, in which the backs of your hands face you. In both grips your thumbs always circle the bar. Once you've gotten the feel of these grips, and have confidence in their strength . . .

. . . you can start learning one of the simpler stunts. As a safeguard against slips or falls, while learning you'll want to use a spotter and keep plenty of mats under the bar. For your first stunt . . .

25

FRONT SUPPORT MOUNT

. . . you might try a Front Support Mount. Begin it from a standing position, with both hands on the bar in an overhand grip. Then bend your knees a bit . . .

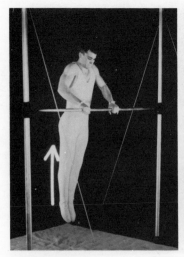 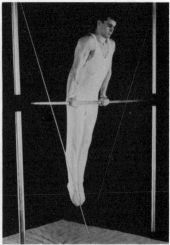

. . . and jump straight up. Pull hard with your arms and shoulders as soon as your feet leave the mat. At the peak of your jump . . .

. . . quickly straighten your arms so that they support your full weight. Practice the Front

Support Mount until you can finish it each time with your head up, elbows in, hips resting against the bar, and toes pointed down. To dismount, give your legs a slight forward swing.

BACK DISMOUNT

Then swing them back, and at the same time
push yourself back and release your grip...

... so that you drop to a smart landing, bend-
ing your knees to absorb the shock, and extending your arms for balance and good form.
Repeat this basic dismount until you can do it
easily and expertly. After awhile ...

SKIN THE CAT

. . . you can develop the well-known stunt called "Skin the Cat." Start it from your basic stance, holding the bar in a regular grip. Then bend your knees so that you will hang from the bar, as soon as your body is fully supported by your hands . . .

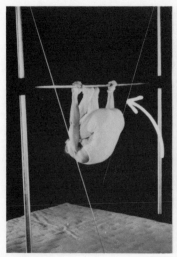

. . . lift your knees so you can pass your legs through your arms and under the bar, extending your legs back through your arms, until eventually . . .

. . . you can lower them behind you to the mat without losing your grip. To finish the Skin the Cat, reverse your movements and return to your original stand. The next stunt you can try . . .

28

SINGLE KNEE SWING-UP

... is a Single Knee Swing-Up. Be sure to use a spotter to guide you through its movements, until you are sure of yourself. This stunt is started while hanging from one knee and a regular grip.

Then bring your free leg up and swing it down hard and under the bar. Take advantage of your full downward momentum to pull up on your arms ...

... so you swing up to a support position on top of the bar. With a little more practice, you should be able to go from this stunt into an advanced one ...

... such as the Single Knee Circle Backward, in which you pitch backwards and make a complete circle on one knee. Or, you can go on ...

SINGLE KNEE CIRCLE BACKWARD

SINGLE KNEE CIRCLE FORWARD

... to the Single Knee Circle Forward, in which you push off toward the front and complete a full circle. Before going into it, however, be sure to place your hands in a reverse grip. After learning the knee circles ...

... you can advance to a stunt like the Back Hip Circle. Start the Back Hip Circle from a front support position on the bar. First flex your arms slightly ...

BACK HIP CIRCLE

... and extend your legs back away from the bar. While you keep a firm grip, let your legs drop naturally, ...

... and swing them under and upward to the other side, of the bar. Pull with your arms through your swing ...

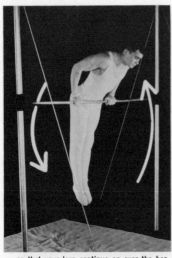

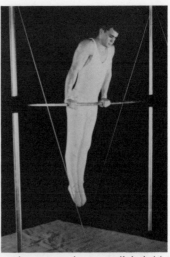

... so that your legs continue on over the bar. During your circle, try to make your hips the pivot point by resting them against the bar and keeping your arms straight. You will have completed your circle, ...

... when you can brace yourself back into your original front support position. Later on in your horizontal bar training, you'll want to put more swing into your stunts.

KIP

One advanced stunt that depends on a swinging technique is the Kip. Begin your Kip with a strong back swing, by lifting one leg back followed by the other.

Then glide both legs forward just skimming the mat. At the front of your swing, arch your back for a second and then bring your legs up toward the bar sharply.

In first learning this you may want to tap one foot on the mat to help lift your feet up to the bar.

34

Now, you're going through two distinct movements—arching yourself out in front and in a flash, piking your body and pulling yourself up. This quick snap-action should shift your weight back and supply enough force . . .

U. S. 1365883

. . . to bring yourself up into a straight arm support above the bar. Concentrate on improving your timing for the Kip, and you will be conditioning yourself for still more advanced stunts . . .

DOUBLE LEG CIRCLE BACKWARD

...such as the Double Leg Circle Backward. Again, for your own protection, have a spotter help you until you've mastered it. Start it from a sitting position on the bar, holding it with overhand grip close to your hips. Now raise your body slightly ...

...and shift your hips back so your knees hook around the bar. Continue leaning back to start you into a circle around the bar.

At the bottom of your swing, when you pass the uprights, start pulling yourself up again. Pull with your swing . . .

. . . and pike your body strongly so you can complete your Double Leg Circle Backward by finishing in your original sitting position. With more practice . . .

SOLE CIRCLE BACKWARD

...you should soon be ready to try a Sole Circle Backward. Start it from a front straight arm support. Then flex your arms and whip your hips above your arms ...

...putting your feet on the bar in a straddle position outside of your hands. Holding this position, fall backward ...

. . . starting into a complete circle while holding on to the bar with your feet and hands. Try to keep an even pressure on the bar with the soles of your feet . . .

. . . as you continue around and toward the top of the bar. When you've almost completed a full Sole Circle Backward, you can continue on over for the complete circle . . .

39

. . . or you can execute a dismount, by releasing your grip and lifting your shoulders and chest up. Then push forward off the bar with your feet and snap your legs under you . . .

. . . so you drop to a smart landing on both feet, your arms extended. After learning a few such dismounts . . .

. . . you can try mastering some of the more spectacular stunts. Your progress may be a bit slow at first. But you'll soon find it's worth all the practice to become a top performer on the horizontal bar.

3

RINGS

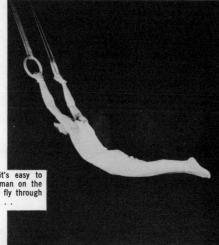

When performing on the rings, it's easy to imagine yourself a daring young man on the flying trapeze. But before you can fly through the air with the greatest of ease . . .

. . . you'll need a lot of training on the still rings. Through the early stages, protect yourself by working out with a mat underneath you. Have the rings adjusted to about head height. And make sure a spotter is available to help you.

The first thing you'll want to do is get the feel of the rings. Test them with a regular grip, your palms facing each other. Then try a simple Chin-Up from a stand.

Later, practice a Chin-Up from a hanging position. Start with your body hanging free and your arms straight. Then pull from your shoulders . . .

CHIN-UP

. . . to raise yourself up into the air in a chin-up. An excellent warm-up exercise, this also develops strength for many ring stunts. With more practice . . .

CHIN-UP
L-POSITION

...you can advance to a Chin-Up with Legs in L-Position. First raise your legs parallel to the mat. And then pull into a chin-up. Still more advanced ...

... is the chin-up with one arm to the side. From a chin-up, while your arms are still flexed, extend one arm out to the side and bring it back. Then do the same with your other arm...

...and return to your basic stance. Repeat it until you feel ready to work up another stunt...

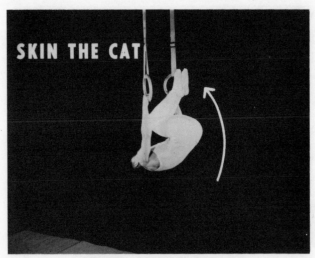

SKIN THE CAT

...the popular one called Skin the Cat. Start by gripping the rings and bringing your legs up. Continue your legs between your arms and into an extended position behind you . . .

...until your toes are pointing downward as far as they can go. Then, by reversing these steps...

BIRD'S NEST

. . . return to your original stance. After learning how to Skin the Cat, you can try the Bird's Nest. Start it with a chin-up.

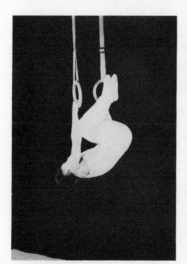

Bring your feet up and over your head as you did in starting to Skin the Cat. Except that you hold at the top of your turn . . .

. . . and place your insteps in the rings. Arch out so your chest faces the mat. Hold the position. Then reverse the procedure to return to your original stance. A variation of the Bird's Nest . . .

45

. . . is the One Foot Bird's Nest. After coming to a regular Bird's Nest, extend one foot back, hold, then return it and reverse your movements back to a stand.

Next you can try a Jump to Straight Arm Support. Make sure you're carefully spotted. Start with a good grip on the rings.

Then jump up until you're supporting all your weight with your arms straight near the sides of your body. Practicing this can be good conditioning for still another ring stunt . . .

KIP TO STRAIGHT ARM SUPPORT

. . . such as the Kip to Straight Arm Support. Starting from a pike, kick your legs upward and forward . . .

. . . pulling with your arms and shoulders to raise your body. While you're learning the Kip, a spotter can give you a slight push under the hips.

This should help you continue your kip until you are above the rings in a straight arm support, your arms against the straps. Later on . . .

DISLOCATE

...you can try the Dislocate. Start the Dislocate from a pike. Then shoot your legs up and back. At the same time . . .

...quickly spread your arms out to the sides turning them through the Dislocate action. Then arch your body...

49

... and swing your feet back down to the mat. It's best to first learn the Dislocate on the low rings.

For further protection, be sure to use a spotter while learning the Dislocate...

INLOCATE

... and such advanced stunts as the Inlocate.
Start the Inlocate by having a spotter lift one
of your legs up toward a pike position.

Continue your hips up toward the rings and
duck your head, turning your arms inward so
you finish in a pike position.

BACK UPRISE

Next you can advance to the Back Uprise. But before trying it, be sure to raise the rings to a height of about eight feet. Then start the Back Uprise by bringing your legs forward and backward.

Swing them forcefully down and back to give you momentum. As your legs swing back . . .

... pull hard with your arms to raise your body up. Put enough back swing and pull into the movement and you should be able to finish above the rings in a straight arm support position.

Later on, you can try learning the Reverse Kip.

REVERSE KIP

53

Begin it from your basic stance. Then bring your feet up toward the rings.

Shoot them up high above the rings so you can change your grip from a hanging position into a supporting position. Now push up from your shoulders . . .

. . . into a straight arm support and you've completed your Reverse Kip. Once you've mastered these still ring stunts . . .

FLYING RINGS

...you'll find they can be even more dramatic when performed on the flying rings. But before attempting any stunts on the flying rings, be sure to learn how to swing properly.

Practice with a spotter and build your skill gradually, so that you're soon able to dismount safely. Whenever dismounting ...

... try to land evenly on both feet, your knees slightly bent. After working up some of the still ring stunts on the flying rings ...

FLYAWAY

... you can try the spectacular dismount known as the Flyaway. Start it by swinging forward. Beat downward at the center of your swing.

Then let your body ride upward into a back layout position. And at the end of your forward swing, ...

...release your grip, pull your head back, and drop into a smooth dismount. As you come down ...

...snap your legs under and land on both feet for a smart finish. By learning more dismounts, mounts, and stunts—and learning them safely—

...it shouldn't be long before you are performing on the rings with the greatest of ease.

4

SIDE HORSE EXERCISES

A tame-looking mount, the side horse. Yet on this versatile apparatus can be performed some of the most exciting feats in all gymnastics . . .

. . . stunts known as Side Horse Support exercises. Learning them will develop your coordination, your timing, and your strength, particularly in the arms and shoulders. But before attempting any support work . . .

... it's best to first master side horse vaulting. Vaults are stunts you perform while passing over the horse from a jump to a landing ...

... while supports are usually performed as you remain on the horse. They require more strength and endurance. So in learning side horse supports ...

... you'll want to condition the upper part of your body. Always try to work from your shoulders, keeping your arms straight for leverage and balance.

You'll also want to familiarize yourself with the horse itself. Looking at it from your approach side, the middle section between the pommels is called the Saddle. The left end is the Neck. And the right end is the Croup.

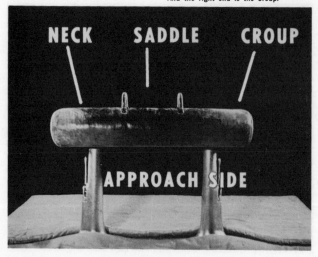

NECK   SADDLE   CROUP

APPROACH SIDE

Yet either end of the horse may be used for performing most support stunts. In starting out, be sure to have mats underneath and a spotter nearby for safety. And remember to practice each stunt carefully and systematically . . .

. . . beginning with a good basic mount. Grasp the pommels in an overhand grip, jump up to a straight arm support, and you'll be in a position to go into any stunt. As you gain more skill . . .

...you will learn to shift your weight from arm to arm, developing a sense of rhythm and timing.

SINGLE LEG HALF CIRCLE

A good beginning stunt you can try is the Single Leg Half Circle. Start it from your basic front support position ...

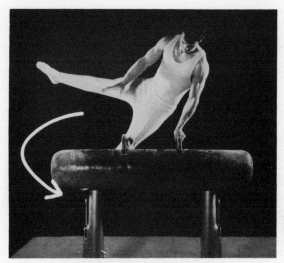

... by shifting your weight to the left, and swinging your right leg over the right end of the horse. Swing it between the pommel and your hand, releasing your grip ...

... and replacing it as you land in the saddle, your right leg in front, left leg in back. Then to complete your Single Leg Half Circle, simply reverse the procedure ...

... until you're back in your original front
support starting position. With a little more
practice ...

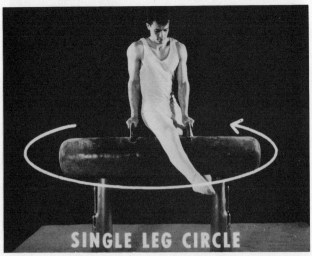

SINGLE LEG CIRCLE

... you should soon be able to perform a full
Single Leg Circle by swinging your right leg
around both ends of the horse. As you bring it
over each pommel, remember to shift your
weight while releasing and regrasping each
hand. Continue your circle around ...

. . . until you've resumed your original front support position. Practicing the Single Leg Circle is good preparation for your next side horse support, . . .

DOUBLE LEG HALF CIRCLE

. . . the Double Leg Half Circle. From your front support, swing both legs a bit to the left . . . and then hard to the right. Bring them over the right end of the horse between the pommel and your right hand.

Continue your swing, sliding both legs along
the front of the horse . . .

. . . until you finish in a rear support position,
both legs between the pommels. Then reverse
your movements . . .

... to complete your Double Leg Half Circle
back into your starting position. For your next
side horse support . . .

REVERSE SCISSORS

... you can try a Reverse Scissors. Start it
from a support position between the pommels,
your right leg in front and left leg in back.
Swing both legs slightly to the left and then
hard to the right . . .

...and over the end of the horse, releasing your right hand and shifting your weight to the left. As you do, quickly swing your right leg back and your left leg forward in a fast scissors movement...

...so you finish back in the saddle with your left leg in front, your right leg in back. Later on, learn to build up momentum for the more advanced stunts...

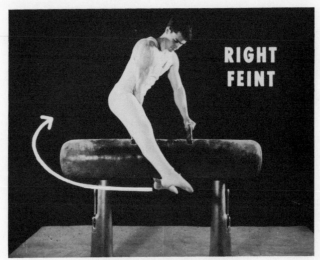

RIGHT FEINT

... by using a Right Feint. From a front support, bring your right leg around the right pommel and swing it back to start you out forcefully into any further support stunt. For example, use the Right Feint ...

SINGLE REAR DISMOUNT

... to start into the Single Rear Dismount. At the back of your right feint swing, pick up your left leg and swing both legs forward over the left end of the horse.

Continue your legs over the horse and come to a neat dismount stand, your inside hand holding a pommel. After mastering the Single Rear Dismount . . .

FLANK CIRCLE

. . . try an advanced stunt such as the Flank Circle. Start it from a right feint, swinging your right leg back and around, and picking up your left leg. Swing both legs over the left end of the horse . . .

... and across the front, keeping your arms straight and hips away from the horse.

Continue swinging your legs over the right end of the horse, releasing your right hand to pass your legs over the pommel until you finish in a front support position. By learning to shift your weight in one Flank Circle ...

CONTINUOUS FLANK CIRCLES

...you should soon be able to do a series of Continuous Flank Circles. Then you can go on to another advanced support stunt, ...

DOUBLE REAR DISMOUNT

...the Double Rear Dismount. Start it from a right feint, bringing your right leg back and picking up your left leg.

Swing both legs over the left end of the horse, releasing your left hand as you shift your weight to the right arm . . .

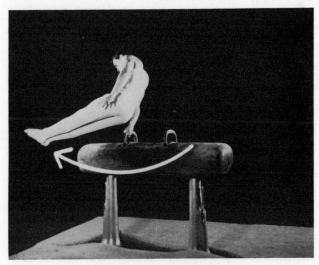

. . . and continue your legs across the front. Keep your hips close to your right arm as you swing your legs over the right end of the horse . . .

... so you finish in a standing position on the approach side of the horse, your left hand resting on the end of the horse. By adding another turn to the Double Rear Dismount, ...

TRIPLE REAR DISMOUNT

... you can advance to the Triple Rear Dismount. Starting again from a right feint, swing both legs around toward the left end of the horse.

Continue them over the left end as you release your left hand and shift your weight to the right hand. Swing your legs around the front . . .

. . . and toward the right end of the horse. As they pass over the right end, keep your weight close to your right hand . . .

...and smartly place your left hand down on the end of the horse. The quick action should shift your weight to the left...

...so you can release your right hand and swing both legs over the pommels...

...then finish by dropping to the mat on the front side of the horse, your left hand resting on it for support . . . and you've completed the Triple Rear Dismount. Later, as you learn more stunts and acquire more skill . . .

...you can go on to develop impressive routines that will show your mastery of this thrilling apparatus activity, Side Horse Support Exercises.

5

SIDE HORSE and LONG HORSE VAULTING

The challenge of overcoming an obstacle, of getting over and around something, is a basic appeal in vaulting. For fun, sport, and all-around development, few apparatus activities offer as much satisfaction as vaulting, whether it's done over a side horse . . .

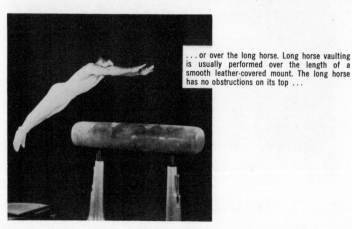

. . . or over the long horse. Long horse vaulting is usually performed over the length of a smooth leather-covered mount. The long horse has no obstructions on its top . . .

... while the side horse is simply a long horse topped by a pair of pommels which are gripped during the lateral movements in side horse vaulting. The side horse can be used for support exercises ...

... but first learn vaulting before attempting any supports. While you're learning side horse vaulting, protect yourself by using a spotter or two, and have several mats around the horse.

Start out by learning a good basic approach to the horse. Learn it in stages. First practice a short running approach until you've developed the right timing and footwork to go into a smooth, balanced take-off.

Next, practice getting a good grip. You'll want to use a regular grip, putting your hands on top of the pommels with the palms facing each other and thumbs to the sides. After you're used to the grip . . .

. . . learn a double-foot take off into a jump. End your approach with a slight hurdle as you reach for the pommels. The instant you grip them, bounce off both feet and leap into the air. Flex your arms a bit as you leap, letting your feet ride up behind you. Once you've mastered the basic approach . . .

FLANK VAULT

. . . you can use it in learning your first stunt, the Flank Vault . . . On taking off, raise one arm, straighten your legs . . . and swing them over one side of the horse. Then release your hand so you land with your back to the horse.

REAR VAULT

Next you can try the Rear Vault. Using your regular two-foot take-off, swing your legs to one side so you pass over the horse in a sitting position. Release one hand for your turn . . .

. . . and then replace it, using that hand to balance your landing. Practice the Rear Vault until you're able to finish it facing the same direction in which you crossed over the horse. Then you can go on . . .

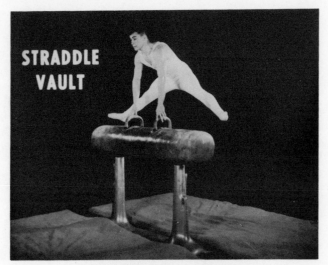

STRADDLE VAULT

...to the Straddle Vault. After taking off from both feet, spread your legs outside your arms and push off hard from the pommels...

...and release your hands, extending them for balance and keeping your head and chest up. Coming down,...

... you'll bring your legs together for a neat upright landing. After mastering these basic vaults on the side horse, then you should be able to try out some of the more advanced ones. And at this point you should have enough experience and conditioning on the side horse ...

WOLF
VAULT

... to try a Wolf Vault. Here, after taking off, you tuck one leg and bring it over the horse between the pommels while sweeping the other extended leg over one end of the horse. Then bring both legs together as you drop toward the mat for your landing.

THIEF VAULT

Slightly more advanced is the Thief Vault. It's done from a single-foot take-off. Start out with your regular approach, and throw one leg up between the pommels. As you do ...

... immediately bring your other leg up next to it so that both feet pass over the horse ahead of you. As your hips pass over the saddle ...

... grip the pommels for a moment with both hands. And push off from them, continuing over for a neat landing. You should be able to do a swift, even Thief Vault ...

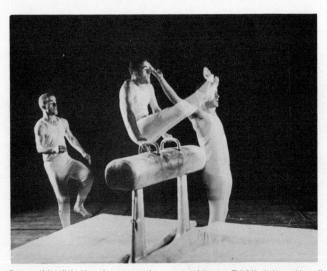

... after practicing it in three key movements: One—approach, lifting one leg and then the other. Two—pass over the horse, extending both legs and gripping the pommels. And three —complete your Thief Vault by pushing off the pommels and landing on both feet, your back to the horse and arms extended.

NECKSPRING
FROM
KNEE STAND

Next, try the Neckspring From a Knee Stand. Start with a jump to a kneeling position between the pommels, in what's called the saddle. Using a firm grip, push up from the arms and shoulders . . .

. . . and lift your hips into the air. Tuck your head in so the back of your neck rests on the saddle. Then lean forward, whip your legs over . . .

... and push off hard from the pommels so you land smartly on both feet. Learn to avoid over-flipping by carefully practicing each move in the Neck Spring From a Knee Stand. Later on ...

... you can try a full Neckspring from a run. Using the basic approach you've learned, run in, grip the pommels, ...

NECKSPRING

... and leap up into the air. Concentrate on getting your hips high so you can bend and place your neck in the saddle. As you come up, try to keep your body in a pike position ...

... maintaining it through your bend. Once your neck is in the saddle, let your hips continue over. When they are past the horse, and you're just beginning to feel off-balance, whip your legs down and push off hard ...

...so you land in a balanced stand on the mat. In first learning the Neckspring, you'll want to practice its key moves one at a time. And after you've gained enough skill and confidence ...

...you should be able to perform all its movements in a smoothly flowing continuous action. Follow the same rule of learning in stages ...

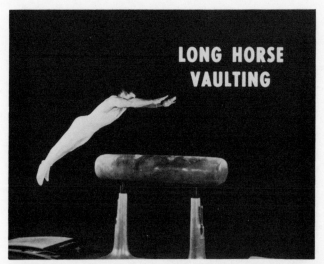

LONG HORSE VAULTING

...when you begin long horse vaulting. You'll remember that long horse vaults are performed lengthwise over a smooth horse. A springy beatboard is generally used to give you the extra momentum you'll need to clear the long horse. So for your own safety . . .

...make sure you have a double thickness of mats at the landing end of the long horse. And have a spotter or two on hand to guide you through your training. Once you've practiced some warm-ups on the long horse, you can try a vault . . .

. . . such as the Long Horse Straddle. Starting with a bounce off both feet from the beatboard, spring up, and forward . . .

. . . and spread your feet into a straddle. As the momentum of your spring carries you forward, put your hands on the end of the long horse and push off hard so that you pass over it and land, feet together. Other Long Horse vaults begin with a similar approach and spring . . .

... but in the Squat Vault, you pass your legs inside your arms in a tuck position and push off hard with both hands to clear the end of the horse for your landing.

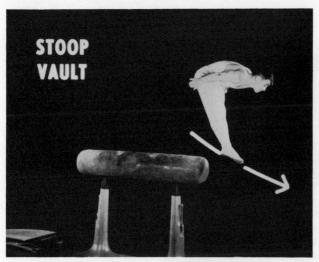

In the Stoop Vault, pike your legs between your arms, and push off the end of the horse into your landing.

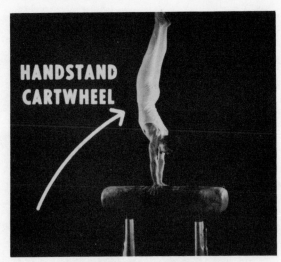

You can eventually try the Handstand Cartwheel, one of the more advanced long horse
vaults. After a beatboard take-off, land in a
handstand position in the middle of the horse...

...and shift your weight to one side, bringing
one hand forward and placing it on the end
of the horse. Continue your cartwheel ...

... by letting your body pass over the supporting hand, dropping you over to the mat for a landing on both feet with arms extended.

HANDSPRING

In time, you'll want to perfect many more vaults, such as the Handspring, both on the Long Horse...

95

. . . and on the Side Horse. But as you do, remember to aim for slow, steady improvement.
For in vaulting, as in all gymnastics and
sports, it's the patient learner who becomes
the polished performer.